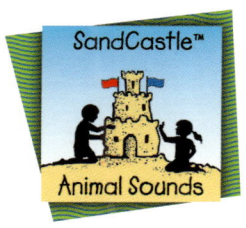

# DOLPHINS CLICK!

### Pam Scheunemann

Consulting Editor, Diane Craig, M.A./Reading Specialist

A Division of ABDO

Publishing Company

# visit us at www.abdopublishing.com

Published by ABDO Publishing Company, a division of ABDO, P.O. Box 398166, Minneapolis, Minnesota 55439. Copyright © 2011 by Abdo Consulting Group, Inc. International copyrights reserved in all countries. No part of this book may be reproduced in any form without written permission from the publisher. SandCastle™ is a trademark and logo of ABDO Publishing Company.

Printed in the United States of America, North Mankato, Minnesota
102010
012011

PRINTED ON RECYCLED PAPER

Editor: Liz Salzmann
Content Developer: Nancy Tuminelly
Cover and Interior Design and Production: Oona Gaarder-Juntti, Mighty Media, Inc.
Photo Credits: Shutterstock

**Library of Congress Cataloging-in-Publication Data**
Scheunemann, Pam, 1955-
  Dolphins click! / Pam Scheunemann.
    p. cm. -- (Animal sounds)
  ISBN 978-1-61613-570-6
  1. Dolphins--Vocalization--Juvenile literature. I. Title.
  QL737.C432S38 2011
  599.53'1594--dc22
                          2010018754

### SandCastle™ Level: Transitional

SandCastle™ books are created by a team of professional educators, reading specialists, and content developers around five essential components—phonemic awareness, phonics, vocabulary, text comprehension, and fluency—to assist young readers as they develop reading skills and strategies and increase their general knowledge. All books are written, reviewed, and leveled for guided reading, early reading intervention, and Accelerated Reader® programs for use in shared, guided, and independent reading and writing activities to support a balanced approach to literacy instruction. The SandCastle™ series has four levels that correspond to early literacy development. The levels are provided to help teachers and parents select appropriate books for young readers.

Emerging Readers
(no flags)

Beginning Readers
(1 flag)

Transitional Readers
(2 flags)

Fluent Readers
(3 flags)

## contents

**Dolphins** .................................................................. 3
**Glossary** .................................................................. 24
**Dolphin Around the World** ........................................ 24

# DOLPHINS

There are many kinds of dolphins around.

They make many different kinds of sounds.

Dolphins use muscles in their blowholes to make sounds.

Dolphin sounds include whistles, clicks, and squeaks.

Each dolphin has its own special whistle. It uses it to tell other dolphins who it is. It's kind of like the dolphin's name.

It's almost like the dolphin speaks.

When a dolphin whistles, other dolphins may whistle back.

Dolphins live in water, but they need to breathe air.

A dolphin breathes through its blowhole. It raises the blowhole out of the water to take a breath.

They are mammals that don't have much hair!

A dolphin may be born with a few hairs around its mouth. The hair usually falls out when it's still a baby.

# Their skin is sleek and feels like rubber.

A dolphin's smooth skin allows it to move easily through the water.

**They keep warm with lots of blubber!**

Dolphins that live in colder water have thicker blubber.

Dolphins hunt for **fish** to eat.

Dolphins eat different kinds of fish and squid.

# Their clicks help them find these treats.

Dolphins listen for the echoes of their clicking sounds. This lets them know how far away things are.

Dolphins are really fun to see. Watch them play, and you'll agree!

# Glossary

**blowhole** (pp. 4, 11) – the hole on the head of a whale or dolphin that it breathes through.

**blubber** (pp. 16, 17) – the fat on the bodies of large sea mammals such as seals and dolphins.

**echo** (p. 21) – a sound caused by a sound hitting something and bouncing back so you hear it again.

**mammal** (p. 12) – a warm-blooded animal that has hair and whose females produce milk to feed their young.

**muscle** (p. 4) – the tissue connected to the bones that allows body parts to move.

**whistle** (pp. 6, 7, 9) – 1. a loud, high sound made by blowing air through a small opening. 2. to make a loud, high sound.

## Dolphin Around the World

**English** - dolphin
**Dutch** - dolfijn
**French** - dauphin
**Italian** - delfino
**Portuguese** - golfinho
**Spanish** - delfin